THE GENERALS
OF THE CIVIL WAR

WILLIAM C. DAVIS

Designed by Philip Clucas
Featuring the Photography of Tria Giovan

MALLARD PRESS
An imprint of BDD Promotional Book Company, Inc.,
666 Fifth Avenue,
New York, N.Y. 10103.

CLB 2736
© 1993 Colour Library Books Ltd., Godalming, Surrey, England.
First published in the United States of America 1993 by The Mallard Press.
Printed and bound in Singapore by Kim Hup Lee.
ISBN 0 7924 5555 X

MALLARD
PRESS

INTRODUCTION

There are two enduring images that come down to us from the Civil War. One is of the haunting face of a young boy, hardly yet a man, in his new uniform, about to go off to find adventure at war, and quite probably his death on the journey. The other is of the resplendent, bewhiskered general, outfitted in grand military raiment, glittering in medals and finery, strutting before the camera just as he presumably did before his men as he led – or sent – them into battle.

No general of the Civil War more epitomized the color and panoply of war than P.G.T. Beauregard. Here at left are his sword sash, kepi, epaulettes, trousers, and tasseled beret.

Both images are in large part mis-representations, but the misconception of what a Civil War general officer was like is far the more prevalent. From the moment the war started, right down to the present, spectators and students have argued the merits of this general or that, and debated their campaigns as if campaigns and battles were exclusively the expressions of generals' minds. The reality of Civil War generals and generalship is considerably different.

For one thing, there has always been dis-agreement over just who *was* a general. In the Confederacy, only men formally appointed by President Jefferson Davis can be considered genuine generals, even though many of these did not

3

subsequently go through the process of formal nomination to and confirmation by the Senate. Yet a host of other men took it upon themselves to adopt the uniform of a general and even to call themselves generals, some holding state militia commissions, and others simply "promoting" themselves. By 1862 there were four grades of general in the Confederate forces: brigadier, major, lieutenant, and full general. However, all wore the same insignia, making it next to impossible to identify a general's rank by his uniform.

Chaos of a different sort reigned among Union generals. For most of the war there were only two grades, brigadier and major general. In 1864 the rank of lieutenant general was reactivated and given to U.S. Grant. However, confusion entered the picture thanks to what were called "brevets," essentially honorary promotions given in recognition of outstanding acts, but which were

not recognized for purposes of rank or command. Some 1,367 men were made brevet brigadier and major generals, when their real ranks never exceeded those of colonel, lieutenant colonel, major, and – in a few cases – even captain. Yet when not on the field they could wear the uniform of a general and be addressed as such. Worse, men could hold one rank in the Regular Army and another in the temporary Volunteer service raised for the duration of the war, and brevets in both services! Thus one officer could hold two different ranks in each service, or a total of four different Regular and Volunteer ranks and brevets.

In fact, 583 men genuinely held full rank generalcies for the Blue, while 425 others wore the stars and wreath of a Confederate general on their collars; in all, 1,008. Beneath the stars of every one of them lies a story worth telling.

FACING PAGE: The premier Union general of them all, U.S. Grant, who emerged from absolute obscurity to become the outstanding grand commander of the war. He appears here in the fall of 1864 at Cold Harbor, Virginia, during the Petersburg campaign. **ABOVE LEFT:** Jefferson Davis, president of the Confederacy, kept to himself the prerogative of appointing all generals, with mixed results. **ABOVE:** Abraham Lincoln struggled for years to find the men he needed to lead his armies.

CHAPTER ONE

THE ARMY COMMANDERS

ABOVE: A successful general might be honored with a specially struck medallion, such as this one commemorating George H. Thomas' victory at Nashville in 1864.

One of the great myths of the Civil War is that somehow the Confederacy enjoyed a wondrous advantage of talent among its generals at all levels. The truth is quite the opposite, and looking at the highest level of all, the army commanders, one almost has to feel sorry for President Jefferson Davis, considering the woeful lack of talent with which he had to deal.

Eight men held the rank of full general in the Southern armies, all of them professional soldiers in the old pre-war United States Regulars. Yet only three of them would ever have been likely to have risen to that rank had there been no war, and the rest would probably have lived and died as forgotten men, like most of the rest of the junior officers of what was then called the Old Army.

Ironically, the senior general above all others in the Confederate service was a man still virtually unknown. Samuel Cooper was a living anomaly. A native New Yorker who had spent 46 years in uniform when the war broke out, he probably "went South" because of his ties by marriage to Virginia's prominent Mason family. He had been adjutant general in the Old Army, but never actually rose above the rank of lieutenant colonel. But when Davis made him adjutant and inspector general of the Confederacy, he made him a full general with seniority over all others. But Cooper never had led,

LEFT: Gen. George G. Meade, seated at center, was the last, and best, commander of the Army of the Potomac. BELOW: Meade's presentation sword, the kind of mark of esteem given to generals who succeeded. BELOW LEFT: Samuel Cooper was the highest ranking general in the Confederacy, yet never took the field, and spent his whole war at a desk job in Richmond – a thankless task made worse by Jefferson Davis' constant interference.

and never would lead, troops in the field. He was a desk general from the first day of the war to the last.

Next in seniority to Cooper was Davis' friend and boyhood hero, Albert Sidney Johnston, a real combat veteran from whom everyone expected great things. He had fought in the Black Hawk War, then in the Texas Revolution, where he became general-in-chief, then in the war with Mexico in 1846-48, and after that on the frontier. In 1861 he was a full colonel and brevet Brigadier, and when Davis made him a full general next in seniority to Cooper, he in effect decreed that Johnston should be the premier field commander of the Confederacy. Yet he proved to be largely a failure, and during his brief months in command in the Mississippi Valley the Confederacy lost vital ground that eventually helped lose it the war. When Johnston tried to regain what was lost by his surprise attack at Shiloh on April 6, 1862, he ignored a wound in his leg and allowed himself to bleed to death.

An even more celebrated "might-have-been" among the army commanders was another

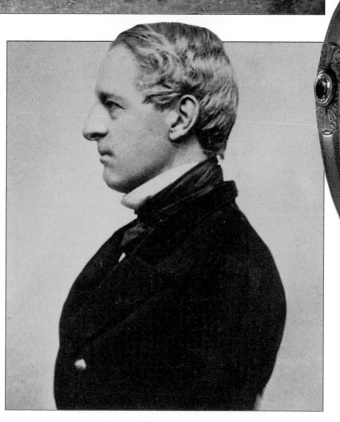

ABOVE: The war's first test of generalship came here at First Manassas in 1861. It was as much by accident as design that the Confederate leaders triumphed. Such early battles were the testing grounds for leaders North and South. It proved to be the first and last big command for General Irvin McDowell, the defeated Yankee commander, but it elevated others like Beauregard and Johnston.

Johnston, Joseph Eggleston. A Virginian who had been quartermaster general in the Old Army before the war, he boasted an exalted reputation that his actual record belied. Following his victory at First Manassas in July 1861 – a victory that owed little to his management – he feuded with Davis over his being ranked below Cooper and others, and then proceeded to demonstrate tendencies that dominated his course for the rest of the war: fear of responsibility, unwillingness to communicate with his commander-in-chief, and an unfailing instinct to retreat without fighting. He came perilously close to losing Richmond in the spring of 1862, before a wound fortuitously put him out of action. The next year he played a large role in the bungling that lost Vicksburg, and then when he took command of the

Army of Tennessee at the end of the year he proceeded to fall back continuously, abandoning North Georgia to William T. Sherman in 1864. When he refused to say that he would not give up Atlanta without a fight, Davis relieved him. Yet so powerful were Johnston's friends in Richmond's power circles, and so limited Davis' alternatives, that he restored him to the command in 1865, when Johnston fell back again through the Carolinas, and finally surrendered his army without authority from Davis. However, in spite of his consistently poor performance, Johnston is still hailed as the untried genius of the Confederacy, due largely to his own boastful memoirs and the promotion of his cause by enemies of Davis, who used Johnston as a tool to further their own vendettas. He was, in fact, a timid,

LEFT: First Manassas made Joseph E. Johnston, but for the next four years he consistently failed to live up to his initial promise. Indeed, he would give President Davis almost continual trouble and frustration as he sacrificed one opportunity after another while consistently keeping his president in the dark as to his plans and movements. A man with an excellent brain, Johnston lacked the force of moral courage and the spirit of self-sacrifice that made several lesser men into much greater commanders. He would be himself one of the principal architects of his inflated post-war reputation, based almost solely on his claims of what he "would have done." Based on actual performance, he rates toward the bottom of the Confederacy's full-rank generals.

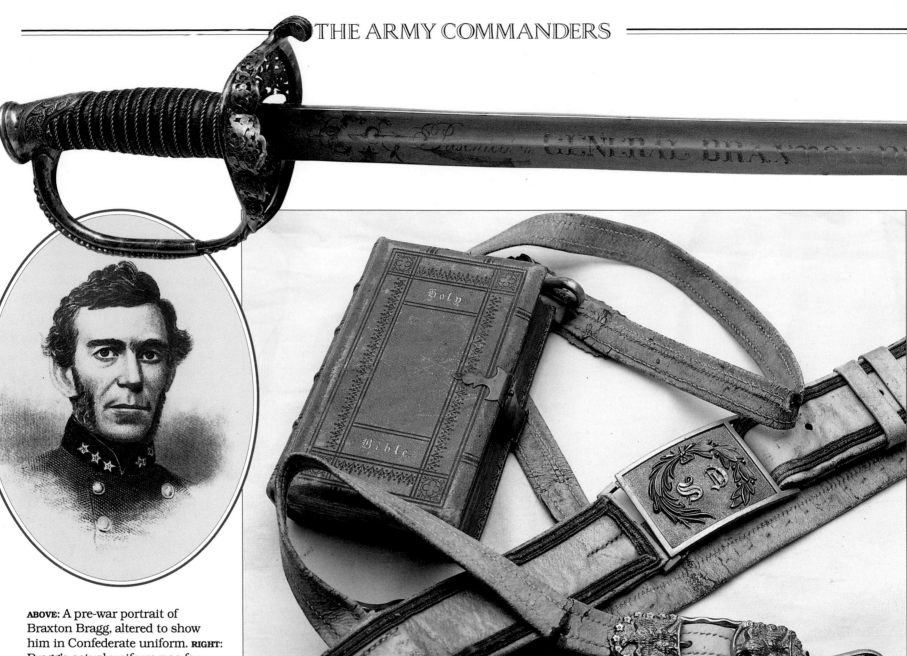

ABOVE: A pre-war portrait of Braxton Bragg, altered to show him in Confederate uniform. **RIGHT:** Bragg's actual uniform was far more resplendent, including this gold-trimmed sword belt. The Bible did not, alas, make him a more charitable commander. **TOP:** Bragg's sword scabbard, simple and unpretentious. **FACING PAGE LEFT AND RIGHT:** Two views of Bragg's uniform blouse, showing the three stars in wreath on the collar, the rows of buttons in pairs, and the four rows of braid on the sleeve, all marks of a general's rank.

quarrelsome officer who lacked the moral courage for high command.

Ironically, the most despised of the Confederacy's high generals, Braxton Bragg, was probably Johnston's superior. He may have been largely incompetent as a battlefield commander, a flawed strategist, and a man so mentally and emotionally ill much of the time that he fought his own generals

more than he did the enemy, but at least he was not afraid to commit himself to battle. The problem was that, once in a fight, he could not control it, could not "read" the progress of events to know when he had an advantage to press, or when it was time to withdraw. As a result, he alternately gave up too easily or pressed on, wasting lives when the battle was already lost. At Chickamauga in September

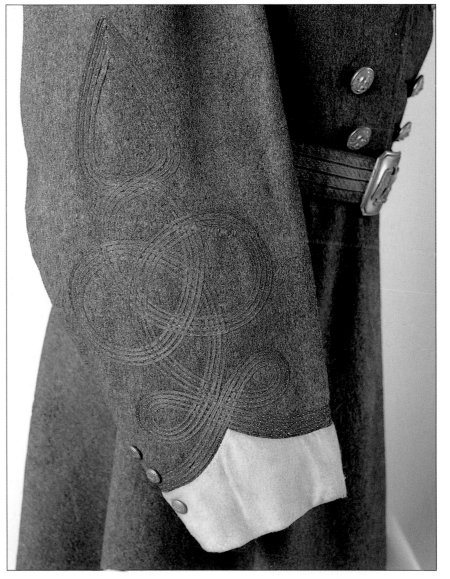

BELOW: "Portici," the Wilmer McLean home at Manassas, headquarters for P.G.T. Beauregard in the only major victory of his Confederate career. **RIGHT:** A part of the Chickamauga battlefield, where Bragg unwittingly won the most stunning Confederate victory of the war. **FACING PAGE LEFT:** The tragic yet heroic John Bell Hood, least able of the major field generals of the Confederacy. He had the heart but not the head for army command. **FACING PAGE RIGHT:** Beauregard. First to last, he was on his own side more than the South's.

1863, he gave the Yankees their most humiliating defeat of the war, then failed to follow it up, and two months later suffered the most humiliating defeat ever inflicted on Southern arms, at Missionary Ridge. Worse, when he lost a fight his first instinct was to place the blame on his subordinates, even if it meant fabricating false charges against them and soliciting perjured testimony.

Of the rest, little need be said. John Bell Hood was made a "temporary" full rank general when he replaced Joseph E. Johnston in command of the Army of Tennessee in July 1864. He proceeded almost to destroy that army by desperate and ill-

conceived attacks around Atlanta, then led it to near-ruin in a campaign into Tennessee that stopped with the debacle at Nashville in December. P.G.T. Beauregard, the hero of Fort Sumter, was at least willing to fight, but he was so wildly impractical in his schemes that they might have resulted in the Confederacy's ruin if carried out. He feuded so venomously with Davis, however, that he never held an important army command after he replaced

BELOW: Edmund Kirby Smith had little claim to being a high commander, yet managed to rise to the top echelon of Rebel generals. More than anything else, he was an administrator and politician in uniform.

RIGHT: Beauregard's uniform blouse shows the fastidiousness of the man himself, perfectly – and somewhat ostentatiously – appointed. The gold braid epaulettes were non-regulation, and worn by very few other generals North or South. The belt plate is unique to Beauregard. FAR RIGHT: The blouse of John B. Hood. He, like Beauregard and others, affected buttons in threes, the old U.S. Army pattern for major generals and above, though Confederate regulations did not provide for such usage.

Sidney Johnston briefly following Shiloh. Then there was the most inexplicable of all, Edmund Kirby Smith. He rose no higher than major in the Old Army, but steadily advanced from lieutenant colonel to lieutenant general in only eighteen months, and to full general a further eighteen months later. He never commanded on the field in a major battle, politicked continually behind the scenes for promotion, then evidenced mortal fear of responsibility every time he got it. Only his blatant sycophancy toward Davis can explain his advancement.

In the final analysis, of the Confederacy's army commanders only one was a truly great general – but how great he was! Robert E. Lee dominated Confederate arms then as he does Confederate memory now. Yet at the beginning of the war he almost missed his chance for greatness, for Davis kept him in Richmond as an adviser. Then his first independent command in western Virginia in 1861 ended in failure, and in his next, in South Carolina, his men derisively dubbed him "Granny" Lee and "Spades" Lee. Lee only got his chance when Johnston was wounded in May 1862, but from then on he

LEFT: The Confederacy's one incontestably great army commander sits between his son and his military secretary. Robert E. Lee sat for photographer Mathew Brady just days after his surrender at Appomattox in April 1865, the fire of battle not yet gone from his eyes. No other general in the South took so naturally to army command; no other set such an unmatchable example of selflessness and sacrifice. To the left is his son G.W.C. "Custis" Lee. He started the war as an aide on President Davis' staff, but won a minor field command by war's end. Standing at right is Lieutenant-Colonel Walter Taylor. Lee liked to have bright young officers on his staff, and military secretary Taylor was one of the best. Lee's lack of ostentation is evident in his uniform. No frills, no epaulettes, no braid on his sleeves. Indeed, his collar insignia is that of a colonel, lacking the wreath around the stars. Nor do his trousers show the regulation stripe. It was characteristic of the modesty of the man.

RIGHT: Mute evidence of the brilliance of a Confederate corps commander, T.J. "Stonewall" Jackson. These ruins of the Yankee rail center at Manassas tell of Jackson's out-foxing of Pope, and the high cost in materiel to the Federals. The August 1862 photo is believed to be by master artist Timothy O'Sullivan.

ABOVE: John Pope was the unlucky commander whose first – and last – battle as army commander was against Lee and Jackson. He also had to fight enemies in his rear, not least George B. McClellan, (standing at right). Like Beauregard, "Little Mac" was first and foremost on his own side; like Joseph Johnston, he had neither the courage nor character for command.

showed what he and his immortal Army of Northern Virginia could achieve. Davis lamented that only one great general ever emerged in a generation, and he needed half a dozen. In the end, all he got was Lee, but he proved himself as good as a host.

By contrast, while few of the Union's army commanders demonstrated the brilliance or flourish of Lee, taken as a group they were considerably superior to their Confederate counterparts. Ironically, with a few exceptions, the best known are the failures – perhaps better known because they failed against Lee – and they are therefore inextricably linked with him. Each of them: Irvin McDowell, John Pope, Ambrose Burnside, Joseph Hooker and, most notably of all, George B. McClellan, failed in the face of the great gray chieftain. Interesting enough, such men had near-counterparts in the Confederate high command. McDowell, like Bragg, was brusque, aloof and disliked by his subordinates. Burnside, like Hood, lacked the brains for his position. McClellan, like Joseph E. Johnston, lacked the courage, and was too prone to play politics in the rear. Pope, rather like Beauregard, was bold, but bombastic and impractical. Hooker was at least a good fighter, but top command overwhelmed him and he lost confidence in himself. Every one of them commanded the Army of the Potomac, or major elements of it, against Lee. Only McClellan, at Antietam in September 1862, gained what could be called a victory over him, and even then Lee bested him in a fashion by extricating his army from a trap that a more daring commander might have used to destroy utterly the Confederate army.

LEFT: Affable, likable, somewhat, bumbling, Ambrose E. Burnside looked like a leader, but that was as far as it went. A good organizer on paper, he was inflexible and unimaginative on the field. At Antietam (below), he wasted lives repeatedly trying to cross "Burnside Bridge" under fire, when the creek could have been waded unopposed a few hundred yards away. Following the debacle at Fredericksburg in December 1862, he would turn command of his army over to Joseph Hooker (far left), who would lead it to ruin at Chancellorsville. He simply lost confidence in himself, and thereby gave up the best opportunity any Yankee chieftain ever had to crush Lee decisively.

Charge across the Burnside Bridge. Antietam. 1 P.M. Sept 17th 1862.

ABOVE: General George G. Meade, able but unsung commander of the Army of the Potomac, in 1864. **ABOVE RIGHT:** Meade's uniform, including his blouse, hat, sword belt and sash, kepi and hat, and his beautiful enamel-and-gilt presentation sword. The epaulettes, as usual, were rarely worn. **RIGHT:** Meade's 1864 headquarters at Globe Tavern, Va.

Not until George G. Meade took command of the Union army in June 1863 did it finally get the commander it needed. He was not dynamic, not flamboyant, not even that likeable to many of his subordinates. But he was unfailingly dependable, unflinching in the face of adversity, and willing to fight. At Gettysburg he gave Lee the worst beating the Army of Northern Virginia ever took in the open field, and he would retain command of the Army of the Potomac until the end of the war, rarely showing brilliance, but an unwavering competence that won the admiration of his superiors and subordinates.

It was from the western theater of the war that the Union's premier army commanders emerged. Not that the region did not also have its share of

FAR LEFT: Abrupt, arbitrary, and a Democrat in a Republican-controlled Union, Don Carlos Buell was disqualified by temperament and politics to last as an army commander. Tactical loser at Perryville, he still forced Bragg out of Kentucky in 1862, but was replaced withing weeks amid accusations – unfounded – about his loyalty and charges – well founded – of being too cautious. LEFT: Buell's replacement was the profane, brilliant, Catholic, William S. Rosecrans, veteran of several minor victories, who gained a narrow victory at Stones River, then lost his reputation at Chickamauga a year later when he panicked.

failed leaders. Don Carlos Buell, commanding the Army of Ohio, met defeat by Bragg at Perryville in October 1862, and was so unpopular otherwise that he did not last long at all. More successful was William S. Rosecrans, who showed some capability in 1862 fighting in Mississippi, and thus rose to

command of the Army of the Tennessee. He fought Bragg to a stand-off at Stones River, Tennessee, between December 1862 and January 1863, but was then routed by him at Chickamauga, and surrendered his position to a successor once Bragg besieged him in Chattanooga.

ABOVE: General Meade sits in the center looking at the camera, while surrounded by his staff and generals in Virginia in 1865.

BELOW: E.O.C. Ord owed his military rise almost solely to his friendship with U.S. Grant. He took command of Union forces in Richmond when the city fell, and here sits with his daughter on the porch of the Confederate executive mansion.

RIGHT: General George H. Thomas rose to high army command despite being disliked by both Grant and Sherman. But his string of victories put him among the most successful of all Civil War commanders. It cost him the love of his Virginia family, who turned his portrait to the wall and severed all future relations with him.

In Rosecrans' place came one of the great commanders, George H. Thomas, a Virginian who remained true to the Union. He was never brilliant, and was often accused of being too slow and plodding. But when he acted, as when he virtually destroyed Hood at Nashville, he could be devastating. Equally unsung were men who led armies west of the Mississippi, like E.R.S. Canby, who accepted the surrender of two Confederate armies at war's end, and showed promise that opportunity never allowed to develop. More dynamic were men like James B. McPherson, who led the Union Army of Tennessee in 1864 until his untimely death near Atlanta, and who was a favorite with U.S. Grant. Other Grant

cronies like E.O.C. Ord and John M. Schofield also rose to army command for little reason other than Grant's patronage.

Two men above all others rose to the heights thanks partly to Grant, but more so to their own talents. The pugnacious – some would say vicious – little Philip H. Sheridan started the war as an obscure officer in Missouri, but by being in the right place at the right time steadily rose and came to Grant's attention. By 1864 he was a major general given command of a small army in Virginia's Shenandoah Army. Showing a positive jugular

ABOVE LEFT: John M. Schofield, another of the less-than-brilliant men elevated thanks to Grant's patronage. **ABOVE:** Philip H. Sheridan, a ruthless warmaker who proved a deadly enemy to foes, whether in Gray or Blue. **LEFT:** E.R.S. Canby, who was destined to fight in the backwaters of the war.

ABOVE: Still a man of controversy after more than a century, William T. Sherman ranks among America's greatest commanders. He had little use for the finery of the army, and was not often seen in his full dress uniform, shown at right, especially with its velvet collar and cuffs.

instinct, he waged a single-minded sort of war to clear the valley of the enemy, and did so with ruthless efficiency.

Even more effective, and probably the most intelligent of all the Union high command, was William T. Sherman. A brigade commander at First Manassas in 1861, he was almost eclipsed when nervous exhaustion practically prostrated him at the end of the year, leading to exaggerated reports that he had lost his mind. Grant saved him, and steadied by the calm, imperturbable guidance of his mentor, the erratically-brilliant Sherman became

LEFT: A scene behind the lines at Vicksburg in 1863, where Grant's reputation was secured. Citizens and Rebel soldiers alike burrowed into these hills, but could not escape Grant's relentless siege.

Grant's chief lieutenant, rising from corps to army command by 1863, and then in 1864 taking over an army group for the conquest of Georgia. Although never exceptional on the battlefield in tactical command, as an overall theater and group commander he was ahead of his time.

Above them all, however, stood the scruffy, unkempt, nondescript Grant, a pre-war failure at everything. He was not as smart as Sherman, as ruthless as Sheridan, as brilliant on the battlefield as others. But he had the overriding quality of unshakable self-confidence and singleness of purpose. He believed in himself and never turned aside from a goal. His rise to become general-in-chief is a pure American success story, as inexplicable as it later appeared inevitable. He led a mere regiment at the beginning, but was backed by influential politicians and good fortune. Surprised in his first army command at Shiloh, he doggedly stood his ground and turned near-defeat into a qualified victory, then swiftly went on to more victories. When he captured Vicksburg in July 1863 he became the Union's premier hero, and stayed such after he relieved the siege of Chattanooga and went east to become general-in-chief, as a lieutenant general. Inevitably he had to come up against Lee, the best in blue against the best in gray. He matched Lee daring for daring, stroke for stroke, and with the aid of unlimited manpower resources drove the Southern giant back into the heart of Virginia to the very gates of Richmond, there besieging him for ten months until the final, and inevitable, last week, when the armies raced for Appomattox. Outnumbered and outclassed in every sort of material as Lee was throughout the war, it took the coming of Grant to beat him at last.

ABOVE: U.S. Grant. No one expected anything of him at the war's outset. Incredibly, he rose above all the rest to the highest rank in U.S. Army history to that time. He did it by a mixture of daring, sound logic, excellent planning, and what Sherman thought was a simple, unflinching confidence in success. When the war ended he returned to a life dogged by failure. War was the one thing he did well.

CHAPTER TWO

THE GREAT LIEUTENANTS

Generals like Grant and Lee did not fight their battles on their own, of course. Indeed, neither of them ever personally led even a squad of soldiers during the war. Their brilliance shone only thanks to their skill in identifying promising subordinates who could take their instructions and translate them into action. It is chiefly among such secondary commanders that the legendary predominance of ability in Confederate gray is to be found. Lee, especially, enjoyed the services of some of the most brilliant lieutenants of the war.

Half of a good subordinate general lay in his commander's ability to "bring him along." None of

ABOVE: Lee's greatest lieutenant, Thomas J. "Stonewall" Jackson. Like Grant, he waged war better than he did anything else, guided by fanatical faith and zeal.

the great lieutenants of the war began at high command. To a man they started in 1861 as brigade, regimental, or even company commanders. Attracting attention, usually for their daring, as captains and major and colonels, they were spotted by senior men as officers of promise. As the armies rapidly grew in 1861-62, and as army organization expanded to keep pace, need constantly arose for good men at ever higher levels of command. Thus such men became among the early brigadiers, commanding brigades. By late 1861 or early 1862 they were rising to major general, to lead divisions. And later that year, when both sides officially adopted corps

organization, these men rose again, and in the Confederacy they became lieutenant generals.

No one was better than Lee at the task of spotting a promising officer and bringing him along, though he had the benefit of starting with wonderful material. At the outset, when he took command of the Army of Northern Virginia, he inherited the 41-year-old South Carolinian James Longstreet, one of the solidest corps commanders of the war. In every battle of the war he gave Lee complete satisfaction, with the exception of Gettysburg, and even there his supposed failures are more the invention of his post-war enemies. Lee rarely complained of "my old war horse," as he called Longstreet, and no lieutenant general ever served him better.

While Longstreet led the I Corps of the Army of Northern Virginia from beginning to end, the II Corps would have four commanders in all. At the end of the war, when it was a shattered remnant of

LEFT: Underappreciated by most except Lee, James Longstreet was a most capable corps commander hindered chiefly by contentiousness and a tendency to politic. His biggest mistakes were after the war when he criticized Lee and became a Republican – twin heresies in the South. ABOVE: Longstreet's dreamed-of independent campaign in Tennessee came to nothing with his attack on Knoxville, which ended in his repulse.

its former glory, the corps staggered behind the banner of Major General John B. Gordon of Georgia, one of the most competent and dashing officers in the service, a man who began the war as a volunteer captain. He had succeeded one of the most colorful, profane, irascible and combative of commanders, Lieutenant General Jubal A. Early, a man whom fellow General John C. Breckinridge said kept his "weapon on edge by sharpening it on [his] friends." While never brilliant, Early had nevertheless shown at times a remarkable gift for combat. His predecessor, Richard S. Ewell, had probably been the least of the lot, commanding the II Corps from May 1863 until the following May, but his skill as a division commander never shone at corps level.

Part of the problem may have been that Ewell and the others had to follow the most fabled of them all: Thomas J. "Stonewall" Jackson. He won a name for himself at First Manassas, and then won legendary status with his Shenandoah Valley Campaign of 1862, defeating three separate Yankee armies with his own under-strength command. Fighting with Lee though the summer and at Antietam, he was put in command of the II Corps

FACING PAGE FAR LEFT: General A.P. Hill's saber, which was with him at his mortal wounding. **FACING PAGE TOP:** The devoutly religious Jackson sometimes led prayers in his headquarters. He stands at left, A.P. Hill sitting at left and Richard Ewell standing third from the left. **FACING PAGE BOTTOM:** Jackson's last successor in command of the II Corps, Jubal A. Early was cranky, contentious, and flawed at high command. Still he was willing to fight and narrowly missed victories in the Shenandoah.

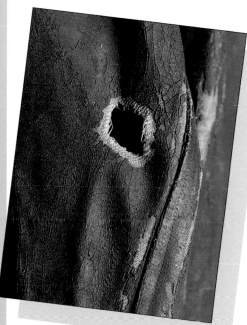

LEFT: Personal items of the great Jackson sit atop a patriotic Confederate songsheet of "Stonewall Jackson's Way." The old high-topped forage cap was not his favorite, but he wore it at times. The spurs were on his boots at his mortal wounding. The white cloth shows blood from his wound. **ABOVE:** The fateful bullet hole in the sleeve of Jackson's raincoat.

RIGHT: One of the most dashing and colorful of the middle level Confederate generals was the gallant John B. Gordon, who began the war as a captain and by its end rose to become a major general and the last commander of the remnant of the proud old II Corps of the Army of Northern Virginia. He became one of Lee's favorites, and in the years after the war a leading champion of peaceful reconciliation and brotherhood. He was also one of the most eloquent – if inaccurate – chroniclers of the Confederate side of the war. FACING PAGE, TOP LEFT: A map of the battle of Fredericksburg, Virginia, prepared by Confederate topographical engineers shortly after the action. It shows the line held by Stonewall Jackson on the right wing of the Rebel position. FACING PAGE, TOP RIGHT: For all of the excellent appointments made by Jefferson Davis, none was more unfortunate and unjustifiable than that of his West Point friend and classmate Leonidas Polk to the rank of lieutenant general and corps commander. There was no more incompetent officer in either army.

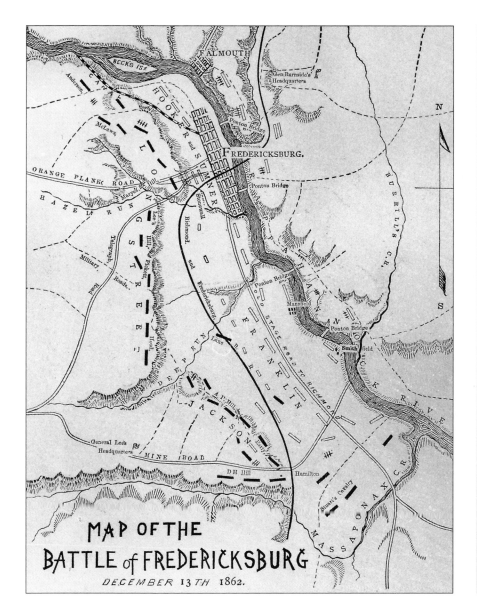

MAP OF THE
BATTLE of FREDERICKSBURG
DECEMBER 13TH 1862.

ABOVE: William J. Hardee, a leading pre-war tactical theoretician, became a corps leader known as "Old Reliable" in the Army of Tennessee.

when it was organized, and led it at Fredericksburg in December, and then at Chancellorsville the following May. There he led it and other troops on the celebrated flank march and surprise attack that routed a Federal army twice Lee's size. The success came at the cost of Jackson himself, mortally wounded accidentally by his own men.

None of Lee's other lieutenants were Jackson's equal, though A.P. Hill came close at times. Put in command of the III Corps when it was formed prior to Gettysburg, Hill gave spotty service until his death in action a week before the surrender. Still, he was far better than most of the men who held corps command in the Confederacy's other armies, for Lee had undoubtedly the best, largely because he trained them himself. The chief lieutenants in the Army of Tennessee ranged from the utterly incompetent Leonidas Polk, appointed to command for no reason other than his boyhood friendship with Jefferson Davis, to William J. Hardee, widely respected, certainly able, but hesitant at high responsibility. A host of others came and went – D.H. Hill, Thomas C. Hindman, Simon Buckner, Breckinridge, Benjamin F. Cheatham, A.P. Stewart – all reflecting the troubled nature of that army from its very inception.

By contrast, though Union corps commanders generally did not show the concentrated brilliance of Jackson or the almost unfailing reliability of Longstreet, on the whole they were more stable and of a kind than the wildly erratic remainder of the Confederate lieutenants. Several were standouts, of course, and those who rose early, like Sherman,

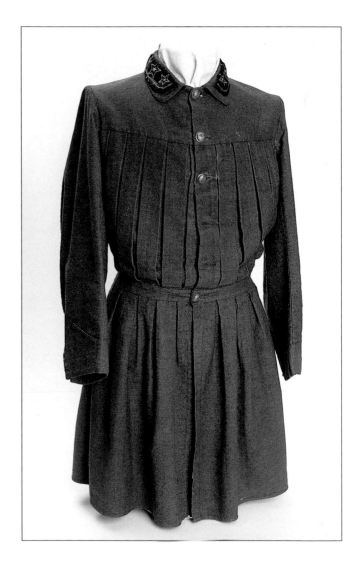

McPherson, Meade and Thomas, ended the war in command of whole armies. Behind them lay a solid core of other men, perhaps only marginally less able. In the Army of the Potomac there were many, their skills unfortunately eclipsed to an extent by their being pitted against Lee and his mighty minions. No star burned brighter than that of John Reynolds, at the head of the old I Corps. Reportedly

FACING PAGE LEFT: The saddle in which Yankee Major General John F. Reynolds was sitting when he was killed at Gettysburg. He was wearing the sword belt and perhaps the sash when he fell.

FACING PAGE RIGHT: Some western Confederate generals wore a distinctive pleated front uniform blouse instead of the more common variety seen almost universally elsewhere. This one belonged to Lieutenant General Simon Bolivar Buckner.

LEFT: Perhaps the Union's premier untutored battle commander was General John "Black Jack" Logan of Illinois. ABOVE: Command of the Army of the Potomac was offered to John F. Reynolds, who turned it down just days before he fell at Gettysburg.

RIGHT: This photo of part of the battlefield at Gettysburg was taken by one of Mathew Brady's assistants less than two weeks after the battle. It shows the area where General Daniel Sickles was severely wounded, losing his leg.
BELOW: Part of the battlefield toll at Antietam, where Sedgwick and other future Yankee corps commanders first showed their capacity for leadership.

he was offered command of the army in June, just before Gettysburg, but declined. Meade assumed the command instead, and Reynolds gave his life on the first day's fighting at Gettysburg, helping hold the line against desperate odds in order to buy time for the rest of his army to reach the field and win the ultimate triumph two days later.

Another man who helped save the Yankee victory did so the following day, July 2. Gouverneur K. Warren helped to hold and defend the most strategic spot on the battlefield, a hill called Little Round Top, and thereby preserved the entire Union position. For that and more services to follow, he won command of the V Corps, which he held almost to the end, until he ran foul of Sheridan the following April. Even more dashing was John Sedgwick, at the head of the VI Corps, who fought with distinction at Antietam and Fredericksburg and into the

Wilderness in 1864. Beloved of his men, he was utterly fearless: perhaps too fearless. At Spotsylvania in May 1864, staff aides warned him to keep low for fear of Rebel sharpshooters. Contemptuously, he declared that the Confederates could not hit an elephant at that range – moments before a bullet slammed into his head.

There were men just as able west of the Alleghenies, and that was where the Federals had an edge at this level of command. Among the several corps that eventually made up Sherman's army group in 1864, there were a number of men who were superior to most of the Confederate lieutenants arrayed against them. Henry Slocum would eventually rise to army command by war's end, having seen service both east and west. Oliver O. Howard commanded a corps both in the Army of the Potomac and the Army of the Cumberland, and

LEFT: Major General Gouverneur K. Warren, who as an engineer helped save Little Round Top, thereby preserving the left of Meade's line at Gettysburg. It won him a future corps command with the V Corps, which he would lose in a feud with Philip Sheridan in the last days of the war. **ABOVE:** Warren's moment of glory, as he stands atop Little Round Top, helping organize the last-minute defense that repulsed Confederate assaults.

would later command an army. Gordon Granger saved the army in the aftermath of the debacle at Chickamauga. Most notable of all was John A. Logan of Illinois. Unlike all the rest, he had no formal military training and was not a graduate of West Point. Rather, he was a prominent Democratic politician before the war, given a commission solely as a recruiting incentive for other Democrats to

enlist for the Union. Yet he steadily rose and showed both competence and combative ferocity. By mid-1864 he commanded the XV Corps, and when McPherson fell in action Logan was next in line for command of the Army of the Tennessee, though he did not get it. Late that year, when Grant was dissatisfied with the slow Thomas, he gave Logan orders to assume command of his army, but circumstances changed and Thomas retained the command. Had Logan actually assumed the position, he would have been the only non-professional of the war to lead a major army in the field.

FACING PAGE LEFT: Major General Henry Slocum, one of Sherman's western corps commanders. **FACING PAGE RIGHT:** Oliver O. Howard would rise to army command.

LEFT: The fence along the cornfield at Antietam, one of the most hotly contested pieces of ground of the entire war. At Antietam and elsewhere Major General John Sedgwick (above), distinguished himself. He would live less than two years, though, until a sharpshooter's bullet cut him down just after he boasted that enemy riflemen could not "hit an elephant at this range."

CHAPTER THREE

THE EXECUTIVES

ABOVE: General Sweeney had no claim to a commission other than his influence with Irish voters.
FACING PAGE: Franz Sigel brought the support of many Germans, but proved incompetent.

Logan was an example of an entirely different kind of general; a kind that achieved and held a largely undue prominence in this war, on both sides. They were called "political generals" and were men appointed because of their connections or their pre-war status as leading statesmen; men whose popularity could be counted on to promote enlistments or bolster the loyalty of wavering states or elements of the population. President Abraham Lincoln, with a much larger and more diverse territory and populace, was perforce required to give more of such commissions than Davis. The largest non-native minority in the North was that of the Irish. Hence Lincoln gave generalships to Thomas F. Meagher and Thomas Sweeney. The largest non-English speaking element was that of the tens of thousands of Germans, especially in New York and Missouri. Consequently, Franz Sigel, Carl Schurz, Alexander von Schimmelfennig, and more, became generals and even corps commanders, with Sigel for a time commanding a small army. Poles were important, too, so Wladimir Krzyzanowski was made a general, though few could even pronounce his name, and many of these generals spoke such faulty English that in the heat of battle they reverted to their native tongues, making things just a bit difficult for their

subordinates. None were competent commanders, but as objects of pride for their fellow immigrants their elevation lured tens of thousands into the Union blue.

Democratic politicians loyal to the Republican war effort, like Logan, also expected their share of generalships. Bumblers such as Daniel Sickles actually rose to corps command, and Benjamin F. Butler of Massachusetts was actually one of the senior generals in the entire service, commanding the Army of the James, until Grant finally managed to weed him out of command. Almost to a man, none of these generals-by-expedience had any military training or ability, Logan and a few others excepted. Their being in the uniform at all was a necessary evil for the greater war effort, but they cost the lives of thousands by their ineptitude, leading Union chief of staff Henry W. Halleck to comment that it was "but little better than murder" to give commands to such men.

The situation was much better in the Confederacy. Davis made far fewer political appointments, and generally better ones. Only a few

ABOVE: Major General Daniel Sickles, seated, shows the price he paid for his incompetence at Gettysburg. Unseen are the hundreds of soldiers who paid for it with their lives. Many of them had been induced to enlist by Sickles and other prominent politicians. **RIGHT:** In 1862, on the Virginia Peninsula, Sickles' men stand in their line. So many of them will fall at Gettysburg that Sickles' III Corps of the Army of the Potomac will cease to exist.

politicians rose to the level of major general, most notably Howell Cobb of Georgia, John C. Breckinridge of Kentucky, and Thomas C. Hindman of Arkansas. All three of these proved to be good choices, especially the latter two. Breckinridge was one of the best division commanders in the west, and rose briefly to corps command, while Hindman did the same, and for a time commanded the Army of the Trans-Mississippi. Neither did Davis have to grant commissions to lure ethnic minorities, for the South was almost exclusively Anglo-Saxon in makeup. He appointed his share of failures, like ex-governor of Virginia Henry Wise, but for the most part, perhaps because he made fewer such appointments, the impact of Davis' commissioning inexperienced amateurs was far less detrimental.

On both sides, many of the amateur and political appointees were assigned to the kinds of commands that best suited their pre-war experience as statesmen and businessmen. For every general leading troops in the field, there was another one whose saddle was strapped to a desk. Both North and South were divided into a number of

LEFT: Politics made stranger generals than bedfellows. The Pole Wladimir Krzyzanowski was well liked, but not much of a general. TOP: Henry A. Wise of Virginia was even less of a commander, and a constant thorn in Jeff Davis' side as well. ABOVE: General Benjamin F. Butler, seated on the chair, was little better.

RIGHT: Meade's capable chief of staff A.A. Humphreys became a major general and a corps commander by the end of the war. Though never an outstanding commander, he was well liked and one of the many able administrators upon whose abilities a modern army depended.

FAR RIGHT AND FACING PAGE: The charge of Humphreys' division in the Battle of Fredericksburg in December 1862. Noted war artist Alfred R. Waud captured the scene for the Northern illustrated press.

geographical departments, districts, and even sub-districts, all of which had to be administered, both to preserve civil order and to provide materiel or manpower support to the armies in the field.

A few such departments were massive, like the Confederacy's Trans-Mississippi, which was literally a third of the nation, and while it had its own small army and a few engagements of note, it was almost wholly an administrative command, so dominated politically, civilly, and militarily by its commander

that it became known as "Kirby Smith-dom." More often the departments were simply the outline of a state or states combined, while in the Confederacy they often came down to those portions of states that were behind current Confederate lines. Occasionally a fighting general like Breckinridge or Simon Buckner commanded such a department, but usually only when it was close to Federal lines and enemy action could be expected to require a commander's combat skills. Mostly the department commanders were administrators like Cobb or Samuel Jones.

TOP: E.P. Alexander served as chief of artillery in Lee's I Corps. ABOVE: Howell Cobb was one of two professional politicians who became major generals in the Confederacy.

ABOVE: General Josiah Gorgas, capable ordnance chief of the Confederacy. **TOP RIGHT:** General Herman Haupt, chief of the U.S. Military Railroad, who kept Lincoln's trains running. **RIGHT:** William N. Pendleton, Chief of Artillery of the Army of Northern Virginia.

Then there was another sort of general: the staff officer. Most of them on both sides were of lesser ranks, usually no higher than colonel, but in a few cases such men wore stars. In Lee's army, the chiefs of artillery of the I and II Corps, E.P. Alexander and A.L. Long, became brigadiers. Lee's chief of staff Robert H. Chilton was also made a brigadier late in the war, while William W. Mackall, chief of staff in the Army of Tennessee, also became a brigadier. Lee's chief engineer, Walter H. Stevens, and his

army chief of artillery William N. Pendleton, won stars before war's end. Out in the far west, Kirby Smith's chief of staff William R. Boggs also achieved a brigadiership.

Staff officers more frequently became generals in the Union services. Grant's right-hand man, John A. Rawlins, finished the war a brigadier. Andrew A. Humphries wore a star while on Meade's staff, and Herman Haupt, Grant's chief engineer and the overseer of the United States Military Railroads, became a brigadier.

Back in the capitals, in the respective war departments, military men not infrequently rose to high rank administering their bureaus. James Hammond wore a star as surgeon general of the

Union Armies. Josiah Gorgas, chief of the Ordnance Department in Richmond, became a general in the last months of the war. So did the quartermasters general on both sides, Montgomery Meigs for the North and Alexander R. Lawton for the South, and the commissary generals as well. And, of course, the adjutant generals, like Samuel Cooper and the Union's Lorenzo Thomas, got their stars, though they never set foot on a battlefield. Theirs were the largely unsung and unremembered problems of paperwork and administrative detail, yet without their thankless toils at their desks the generals out in the field would have had no men, weapons, transportation or clothing, nor anything else with which to go forward and win their glories.

ABOVE LEFT: Lorenzo Thomas, largely ineffectual adjutant and inspector general of the Union army, was sidetracked and replaced by war's end. **ABOVE:** Quartermaster General Montgomery C. Meigs kept the Union armies fed and supplied, setting the highest standards for logistical support of "modern" armies.

CHAPTER FOUR

FRONT LINE GENERALS

ABOVE: John Jones, though not too able, was brave, and like many of the brave, died at the head of his command. FACING PAGE: Union General Jeff C. Davis (left) was a leader who inspired by example.

First to last, the glory boys were the men who led the brigades and divisions North and South. In an era when the men in the ranks expected their colonels and generals to go into battle with them, and when personal example could be all-important in maintaining esprit, these generals had almost no choice but to place themselves at the forefront of their men to lead them into action. For many it was never a matter of choice. Their own enthusiasm and fighting instincts demanded that they be where the contest was hottest.

Such men emerged early in the war, mostly as regimental colonels. Gordon was one, a man with no military experience or training, who proved to be one of the boldest and most effective combat leaders of the war. Leading his Georgia regiment through the fights in 1862, he strode onto the field at Antietam in September hardly suspecting that every Yankee bullet on the field seemed aimed at him. He was hit once, but stayed with his command. A second and a third time he felt the enemy lead, yet still remained with his men. A fourth bullet delivered yet another painful wound, and a fifth narrowly missed killing him, passing through the crown of his hat. Finally, a sixth missile hit him full in the face while he still stood on the line with his men. Toppling over

44

ABOVE: Another view of the Battle of Shiloh. While popular prints like this always showed generals on horseback, sword in the air, in heroic pose, in fact this did not vary widely from the behavior of many battle commanders. **LEFT:** A sketch showing preparation of defensive works on the Brock Road in the Battle of the Wilderness in May 1864. A good general paid as much attention to his men's protection as to leading them into action.

there, too, the armies suffered from the fact that the best battlefield leaders were often among the first to fall, thanks to their necessary personal exposure. Most, however, managed to come through the war, battered perhaps, but alive. Pennsylvania's John W. Geary compiled an enviable record on both sides of the mountains at the head of his division of the XII Corps, and at the Battle of Lookout Mountain in November 1863 achieved a bit of immortality in the misnamed "Battle Above the Clouds."

Over in the XX Corps there fought another colorful division commander, notable for his name if nothing else. Major General Jefferson C. Davis took a lot of teasing for the similarity between his own name and that of his enemies' president. But

LEFT: When General John Jones faced his horse toward the Federal foe in the Battle of the Wilderness, his foot was in the stirrup when the fatal ball brought him down. He preferred death to the dishonor of his brigade fleeing in the face of the enemy. **BELOW**: Part of the area known as the Wilderness, which claimed the lives of several generals on both sides.

no one teased him on the battlefield. When his division along with others was put to rout at Chickamauga, Davis was the only one to rally his men, end the panic, and turn them back to the battlefield where the rest of the army desperately held out. More daring was Israel B. Richardson, whose nickname "Fighting Dick" said all that needed saying. He promised repeatedly that he would ask

ABOVE: Jeff C. Davis, one of the battle-hardened leaders at Chattanooga and other western battlefields. **ABOVE RIGHT:** The summit of Lookout Mountain at right and, in the distance, Chattanooga and the Tennessee River. **RIGHT:** A bird's-eye view of Chattanooga, where men like Sheridan, Hooker, Thomas, and other generals, inspired the Federals to victory. **FACING PAGE:** Yankee General Israel B. Richardson, a front-line leader killed at Antietam.

no man to go where he would not go himself, and he never did. At Antietam he was in the thick of the fight, sensing victory over Lee if only the Federals would push a little harder at Bloody Lane. While trying to make that push himself an exploding artillery shell added his name to the roster of 3,000 other casualties suffered in that bitter battle-within-a-battle.

Perhaps none of them equalled the magnificent Winfield Scott Hancock. At Antietam he commanded a brigade in the old VI Corps, then assumed command of Richardson's division after his

wounding. On every field Hancock distinguished himself, but nowhere more than at Gettysburg. There, on the first day, as the Federal lines were disintegrating and the position on Cemetery Hill was in danger of giving way, Hancock arrived just in time to take command until Meade could arrive. By his very presence, inspiring beyond description, he put heart into his men and steel into their lines. When the commander of the III Corps fell on July 2, Hancock assumed its command. Then, on July 3, with the approach of the massive Confederate assault, it was Hancock who stood in the lines directing the defense that shattered the attack, taking a bad wound himself in the process and nearly losing his life.

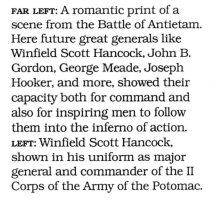

FAR LEFT: A romantic print of a scene from the Battle of Antietam. Here future great generals like Winfield Scott Hancock, John B. Gordon, George Meade, Joseph Hooker, and more, showed their capacity both for command and also for inspiring men to follow them into the inferno of action. LEFT: Winfield Scott Hancock, shown in his uniform as major general and commander of the II Corps of the Army of the Potomac.

CHAPTER FIVE

THE GREAT CAVALRYMEN

ABOVE: Grant's protege, James H. Wilson rose to become one of the Union's leading cavalry generals. In the end he commanded a virtual army of horsemen sweeping across the South.

Even the boldest of the bold, like Hancock, were eclipsed in the public mind, and in the memory of posterity, by a special few who so captured the imagination of the era and posterity that their fame often exceeds the real worth of their exploits. Nothing so appealed to the romantic mind then and later as a man on a horse. The very thought conjured images of cavaliers bedecked in plumes, atop fire-breathing steeds. It is no wonder that the cavalry in both armies during the Civil War, especially in the romance-ridden Confederate service, was self-consciously flamboyant. No wonder that the generals who led that mounted arm, North and South, quickly earned a special place in their peoples' hearts.

Of them all, none would exceed in romance and dash the incomparable cavalier in gray, James Ewell Brown "Jeb" Stuart. He began the war as colonel of the 1st Virginia Cavalry, but even that took a romantic turn when some dubbed his outfit the "Black Horse Cavalry," giving it a sinister, almost brigandish flavor. He showed an early aptitude for the classic task of the mounted arm – reconnaissance, raiding, protecting an army's flanks – but revealed as well a theatrical bent that at times lessened his effectiveness. Performing for Lee, he made one brilliant raid after another, riding around the Yankee army, disrupting communications,

destroying supplies, and gathering valuable intelligence. Quite rightfully Lee thought of Stuart as the "eyes" of his army. But Stuart could not resist the temptation also to plunder, to bring his captures back with him, and to take unnecessary risks for the sake of the adventure, even when they impeded the performance of his actual task. Indeed, during the Gettysburg Campaign Stuart was not where Lee expected him to be, but was off on another raid, thus denying to Lee the intelligence that he desperately needed as he operated in the enemy's country. Still, by the time of his untimely death from a mortal wound in the Battle of Yellow Tavern, on May 11, 1864, Stuart was universally regarded as without a peer in the East, blue or gray.

Stuart's replacement was a different sort entirely. Wade Hampton was a South Carolinian, too genteel

to affect the gaudy plumage and flamboyant garb of Stuart. But that did not mean he did not answer the same impulses of gallantry and daring. At Gettysburg he found himself isolated from his command and facing a Yankee cavalryman at some distance. While the soldier fired his Spencer repeating carbine, Hampton sat his saddle and returned fire with his pistol. Then, when the Federal's weapon jammed, Hampton held his own fire until the jam was cleared, whereupon the two resumed firing, both taking wounds. A year later, now in command of the cavalry corps of the Army of Northern Virginia, Hampton planned the daring "Beefsteak Raid," in which a herd of 3,000 beeves was captured behind Yankee lines and driven halfway around the Federal army besieging Petersburg, to reach the hungry mouths of Lee's army.

ABOVE: The popular image of a cavalry charge is depicted in this print of a Union horse assault at Cold Harbor, Virginia, in 1862. Even more than in the infantry, the cavalry generals led from the saddle.

The Federals, too, had their dashing cavaliers. When Phil Sheridan led a small army in the Shenandoah in 1864, he seemed to have a constellation of colorful horse generals under him: A.T.A. Torbert, Thomas Davies, David McM. Gregg, and, most notorious of all, George A. Custer, a man with a positive instinct for battle, and a single-minded determination to throw himself and his men into the thickest of a fight and trust to "Custer's luck" to see them through. Vain, egotistical, prone to the role of martinet, still Custer was one of the ablest subordinate cavalrymen of the war.

But others achieved greater things, if not greater glory. Benjamin Grierson conducted probably the

LEFT: The premier cavalryman of the Confederacy, J.E.B. Stuart rose from command of a Virginia regiment to a lieutenant generalcy and command of the cavalry corps at the Army of Northern Virginia. **ABOVE:** A romantic depiction of a Confederate cavalryman. In fact, the average Rebel horseman was far less well equipped. **FACING PAGE:** Some of the military effects of J.E.B. Stuart, including his saddle, plumed hat, saber, sword belt, and gauntlets.

FACING PAGE: After Stuart's death, General Wade Hampton of South Carolina took command of Lee's cavalry. The giant Hampton was oft-wounded in action, and just as combative as Stuart. ABOVE: A view from a "crow's nest" observation tower behind Union lines looking toward Confederate lines at Petersburg in the distance. RIGHT: The premier cavalry generals in Grant's command. They are, left to right, Wesley Merritt, David McM. Gregg, Philip H. Sheridan, Thomas A. Davies, James H. Wilson, and A.T.A. Torbert.

most brilliant raid of the war in 1863, when he led barely more than 1,500 men on a back-breaking march south through the entire length of Mississippi in the rear of Confederate lines. It was a diversion to help allow Grant to make his successful envelopment of the Rebel position at Vicksburg, and in the process it destroyed railroads, telegraph lines, tons of Rebel war materiel, and thoroughly disrupted Confederate operations in the entire region. More devastating still was the raid led by

ABOVE: The charge of the 6th U.S. Cavalry on Stuart's command during the Peninsula Campaign on May 9, 1862. In fact, the flashing sabers were seldom used, the soldiers more often employing them as meat spits, and the generals wearing them for show and ceremony.

General James H. Wilson, once a lowly staff officer with Grant, who in 1865 led a small army of cavalry through Alabama in a lightning raid almost unparalleled for destruction by any similar exploit of the war.

It was also Wilson, in the end, who was the only Yankee cavalryman to substantially best the undoubted master horseman of the entire war, Nathan Bedford Forrest. Literally an untutored genius of war – he was marginally literate, though extremely intelligent – Forrest began the war a

private in the 7th Tennessee Cavalry. By 1865 he was a lieutenant general commanding a small army of cavalry, and behind him lay a series of the most stunning defeats ever suffered by Yankee horsemen during the war. Time after time he appeared where it seemed he could not possibly be, defeated numbers considerably superior to his own, then reappeared somewhere else to wreak more havoc. "That devil Forrest," he was called by his foes, and in 1864 Sherman detached inordinate men and means to try to stop – unsuccessfully – his depredations on

FAR LEFT: An example of the penchant of some cavalry generals for show and resplendance. Federal General A.T.A. Torbert displays glorious facial whiskers.
LEFT: Perhaps the most gifted natural combat leader of all horsemen, Nathan Bedford Forrest rose from obscurity to become the most feared of Rebel mounted leaders.

Union supply and communications. Frighteningly fearless himself, Forrest personally killed more of his foes than any other general on either side, and even killed one of his own officers in a fight – after the officer had already shot him in the abdomen. There was no dash, no dress parade finery about Forrest and his command; just cold, calculated, ruthless daring and efficiency. Opinions will always vary, but many would argue that he was, taken all in all, the greatest cavalryman who ever lived.

Thus they are remembered as the greatest, the boldest, the most colorful, and so on. The generals blue and gray have never released their grip on the human imagination, and probably never will. Whether patriots or poltroons, courageous or cowardly, they were what the public saw and most identified with then and later, often to the exclusion of the men in the ranks who bore the brunt of the battle. Yet it has always been so, a phenomenon that detracts not at all from the fact that these few special men deserve to be remembered.

ABOVE: A silver cup belonging to Nathan Bedford Forrest. Such trappings were out of the ordinary for a man more given to drinking from a rude canteen.

CREDITS TO ILLUSTRATIONS
The publishers wish to thank the following individuals and organizations for granting permission to
reproduce the illustrations used in this book:
The Bettmann Archive; Civil War Museum and Library; Colour Library Books;
Confederate Hall and Museum; Tria Giovan; Library of Congress; National Archives;
The Naval Historical Center; Museum of the Confederacy;
U.S. Army Military Historical Institute, Carlisle, PA; Virginia Military Institute Museum

ABOVE: Major General Joseph Hooker may not have been the best of the war's generals, but in looks, in daring, and in bravery, he was not unlike the rest. Patriots, poltroons, and everything in between, they gave both color and command to their armies.